The BIG IDAHO REPRODUCIBLE Activity Book!

BY CAROLE MARSH

This activity book has material which correlates with
the Idaho learning standards.

At every opportunity, we have tried to relate information to
the Idaho History and Social Science, English, Science, Math,
Civics, Economics, and Computer Technology directives.

For additional information, go to our websites:
www.idahoexperience.com or **www.gallopade.com.**

Correlates with Idaho's™
SSAS
Social Studies
Achievement Standards

GALL●PADE
INTERNATIONAL

Reading
Reference
Research
Reinforcement

The Big Activity Book Team

Billie Walburn

Michael Marsh

Antoinette Miller

Michele Yother

Carole Marsh

Steven Saint-Laurent

Bob Longmeyer

Kathy Zimmer

Pam Dufresne

Chad Beard

Cranston Davenport

Shery Kearney

Sherry Moss

Cecil Anderson

Pat Newman

Jackie Clayton

Terry Briggs

Victoria DeJoy

Al Fortunatti

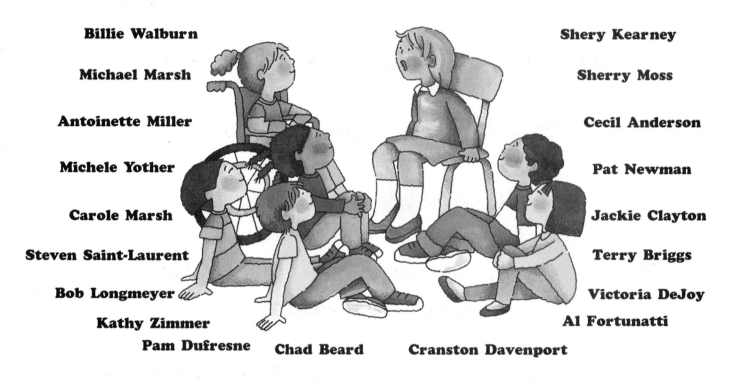

Permission is hereby granted to the individual purchaser or classroom teacher to reproduce materials in this book for non-commercial individual or classroom use only.

Reproduction of these materials for an entire school or school system is strictly prohibited.

Gallopade is proud to be a member of these educational organizations and associations:

Published by

GALL**O**PADE™
INTERNATIONAL

800-536-2GET
www.gallopade.com

SHOPA MEMBER™
School, Home, & Office Products Association

NSSEA

ASCD

The Idaho Experience Series

My First Pocket Guide to Idaho!

The Idaho Coloring Book!

My First Book About Idaho!

Idaho Jeopardy: Answers and Questions About Our State

Idaho "Jography!": A Fun Run Through Our State

The Idaho Experience! Sticker Pack

The Idaho Experience! Poster/Map

Discover Idaho CD-ROM

Idaho "GEO" Bingo Game

Idaho "HISTO" Bingo Game

A Word From The Author

Idaho is a very special state. Almost everything about Idaho is interesting and fun! It has a remarkable history that helped create the great nation of America. Idaho enjoys an amazing geography of incredible beauty and fascination. The state's people are unique and have accomplished many great things.

This Activity Book is chock-full of activities to entice you to learn more about Idaho. While completing puzzles, coloring activities, word codes, and other fun-to-do activities, you'll learn about your state's history, geography, people, places, animals, legends, and more.

Whether you're sitting in a classroom, stuck inside on a rainy day, or—better yet—sitting in the back seat of a car touring the wonderful state of Idaho, my hope is that you have as much fun using this Activity Book as I did writing it.

Enjoy your Idaho Experience—it's the trip of a lifetime!!

Carole Marsh

Geographic Tools

Beside each geographic need listed, put the initials of the tool that can best help you!

(CR) Compass Rose   (LL) Longitude and Latitude
(M) Map   (G) Grid
(K) Map key/legend

1. _____ I need to find the geographic location of Germany.

2. _____ I need to learn where an airport is located in Boise.

3. _____ I need to find which way is north.

4. _____ I need to chart a route from Idaho to California.

5. _____ I need to find a small town on a map.

Match the items on the left with the items on the right.

1. Grid system
2. Compass rose
3. Longitude and latitude
4. Two of Idaho(s) borders
5. Symbols on a map

A. Map key or legend
B. Oregon or Montana
C. A system of letters and numbers
D. Imaginary lines around the earth
E. Shows N, S, E, and W

ANSWERS: 1-LL; 2-K; 3-CR; 4-M; 5-G; 1-C; 2-E; 3-D; 4-B; 5-A

Hells Canyon

The Snake River forms not only the border between Idaho and Oregon, but it also formed Hells Canyon! It took the Snake River more than one million years to cut through the volcanic rock and form the deepest gorge in North America. Hells Canyon is more then 7,000 feet (2,135 meters) deep at some locations. The deepest spot plunges 8,032 feet (2,450 meters)-1/3 mile (0.5 kilometers) deeper than the Grand Canyon! The canyon is 150 miles (168 kilometers) long and includes more than 67 miles (107 kilometers) of the Snake River.

Hells Canyon is home to a large variety of animals including large birds, bighorn sheep, cougars, coyotes, and black bears.

The best view in the canyon is from Sheep Rock in Seven Devils Mountains. Nez Perce legend says the father of their tribe, Coyote, dug Hells Canyon in one day to keep his people safe from the evil Seven Devils!

1. How long did it take the Snake River to form Hells Canyon?

_____

2. How long is Hells Canyon?

_____

3. How long have Native Americans lived in Hells Canyon?

_____

4. How deep is the deepest point in Hells Canyon?

_____

5. Where can people see the best view of Hells Canyon?

_____

ANSWERS: 1-more than a million years; 2-150 miles; 3-more than 8,000 years; 4-8,032 feet; 5-Sheep Rock

Idaho Government

Idaho's state government, just like our national government, is made up of three branches. Each branch has a certain job to do. Each branch also has some power over the other branches. We call this system checks and balances. The three branches work together to make our government work smoothly.

Executive Branch	Legislative Branch	Judicial Branch
A governor, lieutenant governor, secretary of state, controllor, treasurer, superintendent of public instruction, and attorney general	Idaho's legislative branch has two houses. The senate has 35 members and the house of representatives has 70 members.	Idaho's Supreme Court has five justices. Lesser courts include court of appeals, district court, and magistrate court.

For each of these government officials, circle whether he or she is part of the EXECUTIVE, the LEGISLATIVE, or the JUDICIAL branch.

1. the governor   EXECUTIVE   LEGISLATIVE   JUDICIAL

2. chief justice of the Supreme Court   EXECUTIVE   LEGISLATIVE   JUDICIAL

3. attorney general   EXECUTIVE   LEGISLATIVE   JUDICIAL

4. speaker of the House of Representatives   EXECUTIVE   LEGISLATIVE   JUDICIAL

5. a state senator   EXECUTIVE   LEGISLATIVE   JUDICIAL

6. a state representative   EXECUTIVE   LEGISLATIVE   JUDICIAL

7. the attorney general   EXECUTIVE   LEGISLATIVE   JUDICIAL

8. secretary of state   EXECUTIVE   LEGISLATIVE   JUDICIAL

9. probate court judge   EXECUTIVE   LEGISLATIVE   JUDICIAL

10. chairman of the state senate   EXECUTIVE   LEGISLATIVE   JUDICIAL

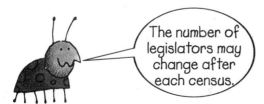

The number of legislators may change after each census.

ANSWERS: 1-executive; 2-judicial; 3-executive; 4-legislative; 5-legislative; 6-legislative; 7-executive; 8-executive; 9-judicial; 10-executive

All Around Idaho! Bubblegram

Bubble up on your knowledge of Idaho's bordering states.

Fill in the bubblegram by using the clues below.

1. State that shares most of the Snake River with Idaho
2. A state east of Idaho
3. A state west of Idaho
4. A state to the southwest of Idaho
5. A state to the southeast of Idaho

1. __ __ ◯ ◯ __ __

2. ◯ __ __ __ __ __ ◯

3. __ __ ◯ __ __ __ __ __ ◯ __ __

4. __ ◯ __ __ __

5. __ ◯ __ __

Now unscramble the "bubble" letters to find out the mystery words!

Hint: Idaho is also known as the _____ _____.

MYSTERY WORDS: __ __ __ __ __ __ __ __

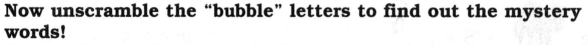

City of Trees!

Idaho's capital city got its name from the cottonwoods, willows, and birches that line the Boise River. According to the legend, French Canadian fur trappers journeyed through Idaho's desert when they saw the trees and cried "Les bois! Les bois!" *Bois*, which means "trees" in French, eventually became Boise.

In 1863, Boise was founded as a farming and supply center for the mining towns in the area. It was the only town in the area that supported family life. Within a year, Boise became the territorial capital. Many of the buildings built during the city's first five years are still standing. Today, it is the largest city in the northern Rocky Mountains.

1. The  is a series of parks connected by foot and bike paths.

2. Convicts built the  + IARY, which operated for more than a century and is on the National Register of Historic Places.

3. To catch a ride on the Boise Tour Train, go to 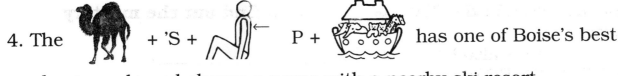 Village.

4. The 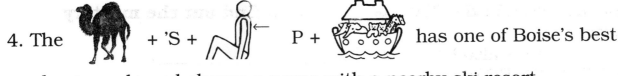 has one of Boise's best playgrounds and shares a name with a nearby ski resort.

Idaho Wheel of Fortune, Indian Style!

The names of Idaho's many Native American tribes contain enough consonants to play . . . Wheel of Fortune!

See if you can figure out the Wheel of Fortune-style puzzles below! "Vanna" has given you some of the consonants in each word.

S H _ S H _ S H _ N _

N _ N Z _ P _ R C _

C _ _ _ R _ D' _ L _ N _

P _ N D _ D' _ R _ _ L L _

K _ _ T _ N _ _

B _ N N _ C K

P _ _ _ _ T

Rainbow, Pretty Rainbow

Rainbows often appear over Borah Peak after a storm. Rainbows are formed when sunlight bends through raindrops. Big raindrops produce the brightest, most beautiful rainbows. You can see rainbows early or late on a rainy day when the sun is behind you.

Color the rainbow in the order the colors are listed below, starting at the top of the rainbow. Then, in each band write down as many Idaho-related words as you can think of that begin with the same first letter as that color!

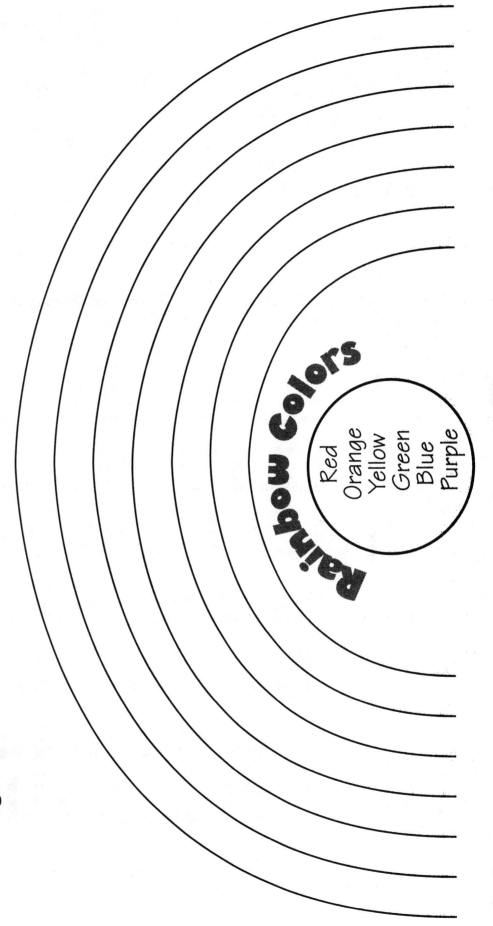

Rainbow Colors

Red
Orange
Yellow
Green
Blue
Purple

In the Beginning... There Were Explorers

Meriwether Lewis and William Clark and the Corps of Discovery entered Idaho in 1805 through Lemhi Pass when they were exploring the Louisiana Territory from St. Louis, Missouri, to the Pacific Ocean. Their news about the area's wildlife spread quickly, and fur trappers headed to the Northwest. David Thompson, a British-Canadian trapper and surveyor, established the first trading post in Idaho in 1809, Kullyspell House at Lake Pend Oreille.

Help Lewis and Clark find their way to the Snake River!

U.S. Time Zones

Would you believe that the contiguous United States is divided into four time zones? It is! Because of the rotation of the earth, the sun appears to travel from east to west. Whenever the sun is directly overhead, we call that time noon. When it is noon in Atlanta, Georgia, the sun has a long way to go before it is directly over Lewiston, Idaho. There is a one-hour time difference between each zone!

Idaho is split into two different time zones-the Mountain zone and the Pacific zone. There is a one-hour time difference between each zone! When it is 12:00 p.m. (noon) in Lewiston, Idaho, it is 1 p.m. in Montpelier, Idaho. When its is 9 p.m. Nordman, Idaho, it is 10 p.m. in Burley, Idaho.

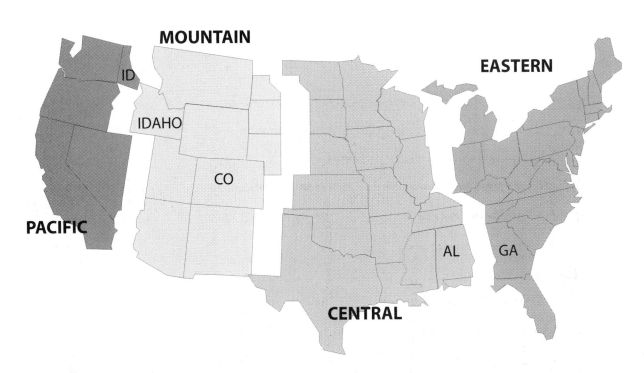

Look at the time zones on the map below then answer the following questions:

1. When it is 10:00 a.m. in Coeur d'Alene, Idaho what time is it in California?
    _____ a.m.

2. When it is 3:30 p.m. in Atlanta, Georgia, what time is it in Preston, Idaho?
    _____ p.m.

3. In what time zones is Idaho located? _____

4. In what time zone is Colorado located? _____

5. If it is 10:00 p.m. in Malad City, Idaho, what time is it in Alabama?
    _____ p.m.

ANSWERS: 1-10:00 a.m.; 2-1:30 p.m.; 3-Mountain and Pacific; 4-Mountain; 5-11 p.m.

Sing Like an Idaho Bird Word Jumble

Arrange the jumbled letters in the proper order for the names of birds found in Idaho.

WORD BANK

blue heron	prairie chicken
duck	red-tailed hawk
golden eagle	trumpeter swan
mountain bluebird	western tanager
partridge	

dcku __ __ __ __

uelb ehnro __ __ __ __   __ __ __ __ __

inaoumnt rdlbebui __ __ __ __ __ __ __ __   __ __ __ __ __ __ __ __

ernwset angetar __ __ __ __ __ __ __   __ __ __ __ __ __ __

tmterurpe wasn __ __ __ __ __ __ __ __ __   __ __ __ __

olgedn alege __ __ __ __ __ __   __ __ __ __ __

edr-edaitl whka __ __ __-__ __ __ __ __ __   __ __ __ __

aipreri khicnce __ __ __ __ __ __ __   __ __ __ __ __ __ __

arptgeid __ __ __ __ __ __ __ __ __

Idaho Schools Rule!

Missionaries established the first schools in Idaho to convert the Native Americans. In 1837, the first school for Native American children was established by Henry Spalding at the Lapwai Mission. The first school for settlers' children was established in 1860 in Franklin by the Mormons. In 1882, Idaho's first high school opened in Boise.

The University of Idaho at Moscow was chartered in 1889 and is the largest of the state's public universities. Other state universities include Idaho State University at Pocatello, Boise State University, and Lewis-Clark University at Lewiston. Private colleges in the state include Albertson (formerly the College of Idaho) at Caldwell, Northwest Nazarene College at Nampa, and Ricks College at Rexburg.

Complete the names of these Idaho schools. Use the Word Bank to help you. Then, use the answers to solve the code at the bottom.

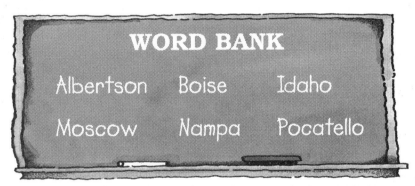

WORD BANK

| Albertson | Boise | Idaho |
| Moscow | Nampa | Pocatello |

1. Idaho State University at __ __ __ __ __ __ __ __ __
             3

2. __ __ __ __ __ State University
  2

3. University of __ __ __ __ __ at __ __ __ __ __
         1   5

4. __ __ __ __ __ __ __ __ __ College at Caldwell
  7 4

5. Northwest Nazarene College at __ __ __ __ __
                              6

The coded message tells you what all college students want!

__ __ __ __ __ __ __
1 2 3 4 5 6 7

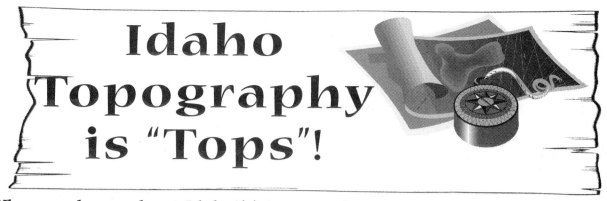

Idaho Topography is "Tops"!

When we learn about Idaho'(s) topography, we use special words to describe them. These words describe the things that make each part of the state interesting.

Cross out every other letter below beginning with the first one to find out what each topographical term is!

1. R M A O I U N N I T E A R I T N: a very high peak or hill

2. L C P L N I T F R F: a high steep rock that drops down sharply and with no slope

3. C P O L L A U T M E B A I U: a mountain or hill with a level top

4. A C W A C N K Y L O W N: a deep, narrow valley with steep sides

5. B F Y O O O P T L H M I B L X L A S: low hills near the bottom of a mountain range

6. R V I A V L E L R E S Y: a low area of land with a river or stream running through it that is surrounded by higher land

7. Y D R E Q S O E U R K T: an area of land that consists of sand, gravel, or rock with very little vegetation

8. M V O O U L N C T A A N I O: an opening in the earth's crust, often at the top of a mountain, from which lava escapes

9. W L R A D V F A: rock formed by the rapid cooling of molten rock that flows from a volcano

10. Q P G A J N L H Z A X N V D N L Y E: a strip of land that looks like a handle of a pan on a map

ANSWERS: 1-mountain; 2-cliff; 3-plateau; 4-gorge; 5-foothills; 6-valley; 7-desert; 8-volcano; 9-lava; 10-panhandle

Oh! Say Can You See...
Idaho's State Flag!

Idaho's current state flag was adopted in 1907. It features the state seal in the center of a blue field. Below the seal, the words "State of Idaho" are embroidered in gold block letters on a red band.

**Color
Idaho's
state flag.**

Design your own Diamante About Idaho!

A *diamante* is a cool diamond-shaped poem on any subject.

You can write your very own diamante poem on Idaho by following the simple line by line directions below. Give it a try!

Line 1:   Write the name of your state.

Line 2:   Write the name of the state bird.

Line 3:   Write the name of the state tree.

Line 4:   Write the name of the state song.

Line 5:   Write the name of Idaho's most famous underground caverns near Twin Falls.

Line 6:   Write the name of the state fish.

Line 7:   Write the name of your state.

_____

_____ _____

_____ _____ _____

_____ _____ _____ _____

_____ _____ _____

_____ _____

_____

YOU'RE a poet! Did you know it?

History Mystery Tour!

Idaho is bursting at the seams with history! Here are just a few of the many historical sites that you might visit. **Try your hand at locating them on the map! Draw a symbol for each site on the Idaho map below.**

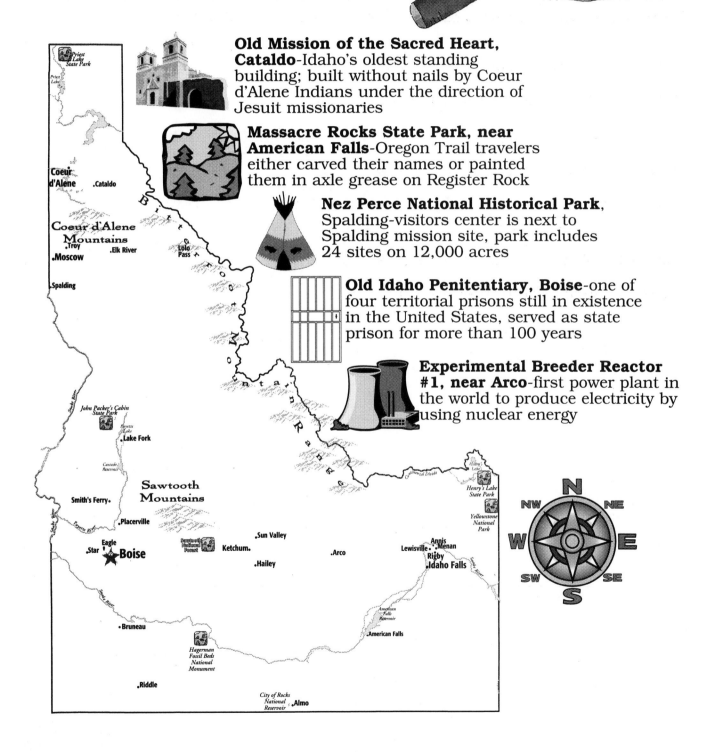

Old Mission of the Sacred Heart, Cataldo-Idaho's oldest standing building; built without nails by Coeur d'Alene Indians under the direction of Jesuit missionaries

Massacre Rocks State Park, near American Falls-Oregon Trail travelers either carved their names or painted them in axle grease on Register Rock

Nez Perce National Historical Park, Spalding-visitors center is next to Spalding mission site, park includes 24 sites on 12,000 acres

Old Idaho Penitentiary, Boise-one of four territorial prisons still in existence in the United States, served as state prison for more than 100 years

Experimental Breeder Reactor #1, near Arco-first power plant in the world to produce electricity by using nuclear energy

What in the World?

A hemisphere is one-half of a sphere (globe) created by the prime meridian or equator. Every place in the world is in two hemispheres (Northern or Southern and Eastern or Western). The equator is an imaginary line that runs around the world from left to right and divides the globe into the Northern Hemisphere and the Southern Hemisphere. The prime meridian is an imaginary line that runs around the world from top to bottom and divides the globe into the Eastern Hemisphere and Western Hemisphere.

Label the Northern and Southern Hemispheres.

Write E on the equator.

Is Idaho in the NORTHERN or SOUTHERN Hemisphere? (circle one)

Color the map.

Label the Eastern and Western Hemispheres.

Write PM on the prime meridian.

Is Idaho in the EASTERN or WESTERN Hemisphere? (circle one)

Color the map.

Interesting Idaho!

Idaho has so many cool places to go and so many cool things to do!

Use the Word Bank to help you complete the sentences below and learn about some of the exciting Idaho sites you can visit!

1. Old Fort Boise in __ __ __ __ __ is an exact replica of an 1834 trading post.

2. __ __ __ __ __ __ City, War Eagle Mountain, east of Murphy, is Idaho's best-preserved ghost town.

3. Shoshone Falls, near __ __ __ __ __ __ __ __, is nicknamed the "Niagara of the West."

4. __ __ __ __ River Battleground, near Preston, is the site of the 1863 Battle of Bear River between Shoshone Indians and federal soldiers.

5. Battle of White Bird __ __ __ __ __ __, near Grangeville, is the site of the opening battle of the Nez Perce War.

6. The Thomas Sleight __ __ __ __ __, built in 1863, in Paris was the first building in Bear Lake valley.

7. Fossils of early horses, mastodons, saber-tooth tigers, and more have been found at __ __ __ __ __ __ __ __ Fossil Beds National Monument in Hagerman.

8. __ __ __ __ __ __ __ __ __ Monument in Tendoy honors the Indian woman who guided and helped the Meriwether Lewis and William Clark expedition.

WORD BANK

Bear	Cabin	Canyon	Hagerman
Parma	Sacajawea	Silver	Shoshone

Please Come to Idaho!

You have a friend who lives in Georgia. She is thinking of moving to Idaho because she wants to be a ski instructor, and Idaho is home to some of the world's best ski resorts.

Write your friend a letter describing Idaho and some of the ski instructor opportunities here.

Skiers from around the world head to Idaho's Wood River Valley in the winter. Towns in the area include Sun Valley, Ketchum, River Run, Elkhorn, and Warm Springs. Sun Valley is a world-renowned ski resort and often hosts world-class ice skaters and skiers. Summer activities include horseback riding, paragliding, mountain biking, fishing, and boating.

This Spud's for You!

Idaho is paradise for potatoes. More than 500 square miles (1,295 square kilometers) of the state are planted in potatoes. In May and June, the potato's vinelike leaves and yellow flowers can be seen along the backroads of the Snake River Valley.

Potatoes are tubers (swollen roots) that grow in bunches under the ground. The combination of the state's light, moist volcanic soil, hot days, cold nights, and water from melting snow in nearby mountains make Idaho's potatoes a taste treat.

Potatoes are native to the Andes Mountains of Bolivia and Peru. The potato made its way to Europe after Spanish conquistadors overran the Incan Empire. Immigrants to the United States brought potatoes with them during the early 19th century.

Idaho is most famous for the Russet Burbank potato. Luther Burbank, a pioneer in plant experimentation, developed the original seedlings in the 1870s.

Idaho is the leading producer of the versatile vegetable in the United States and grows about one-third of the nation's potato crop. To make sure you are buying genuine Idaho potatoes, look for the "Grown in Idaho" seal.

1. Potatoes are _____ that grow underground. (DOWN)

2. _____ brought potatoes to the United States. (ACROSS)

3. Potatoes originally came from the _____ Mountains of Bolivia and Peru. (ACROSS)

4. Idaho's most well known potato is the _____ _____. (ACROSS)

5. The "Grown in Idaho" seal means potatoes are _____ Idaho potatoes (DOWN)

ANSWERS: 1-tubers; 2-Immigrants; 3-Andes; 4-Russet Burbank; 5-genuine

Idaho Rules!

The 1890 Great Northern Railroad Preserve Act provided for railroad construction from St. Paul, Minnesota, to Seattle, Washington, through northern Idaho.

Use the code to complete the sentences.

A	B	C	D	E	F	G	H	I	J	K	L	M	N	O	P
1	2	3	4	5	6	7	8	9	10	11	12	13	14	15	16

Q	R	S	T	U	V	W	X	Y	Z
17	18	19	20	21	22	23	24	25	26

1. State rules are called __ __ __ __.
   12 1 23 19

2. Laws are made in our state __ __ __ __ __ __ __.
   3 1 16 9 20 15 12

3. The leader of our state is the __ __ __ __ __ __ __ __.
   7 15 22 5 18 14 15 18

4. We live in the state of __ __ __ __ __.
   9 4 1 8 15

   National Wild and Scenic Rivers Act in 1968 preserved sections of Idaho's wilderness.

5. The capital of our state is __ __ __ __ __.
   2 15 9 19 5

I D A H O ! ! !

Buzzing Around Idaho!

Write the answers to the questions below. To get to the beehive, follow a path through the maze.

1. Shoshone Indians stampeded bison over the _____ Bison Jump, then butchered them at the bottom.
2. Bechler District of _____ National Park near Marysville is on the Wyoming/Idaho border.
3. Craters of the Moon National Monument near _____ is a plain of ancient volcanic lava.
4. Sunshine Mine Memorial in_____ recalls the 1972 mining disaster.
5. Idaho State Vietnam Veterans Memorial in _____ _____ is inscribed with all the names of Idahoans killed or missing in action during the war in Southeast Asia.
6. Balanced Rock near _____ is a rock formation that looks like a giant mushroom or question mark.
7. City of Rocks National Reserve near _____ has granite columns 60–70 stories high.
8. The Menan Buttes are two 10,000–year–old glassy basalt lava buttes found near _____.
9. Sheep Rock near _____ is a 6,847-foot (2,087-meter) National Natural Landmark in Seven Devils Mountains.
10. _____ is known as the "Potato Capital of the World."

Idaho Through the Years!

Many great things have happened in Idaho throughout its history. Chronicle the following important Idaho events by solving math problems to find out the years in which they happened.

1. Members of the Meriwether Lewis and William Clark expedition travel through Idaho
    $1÷1=$ $2x4=$ $3-3=$ $2+3=$

2. David Thompson builds the first trading post in the area at Lake Pend Oreille
    $2÷2=$ $7+1=$ $9-9=$ $3x3=$

3. Fort Hall and Fort Boise are established
    $9-8=$ $6+2=$ $4-1=$ $2x2=$

4. Elias Pierce discovers gold on Orofino Creek
    $1+0=$ $4+4=$ $8-2=$ $5x0=$

5. Idaho becomes a U.S. territory
    $5-4=$ $5+3=$ $7-1=$ $1+2=$

6. Silver deposits found in Coeur d'Alene Mountains
    $4÷4=$ $9-1=$ $8+0=$ $3+1=$

7. Idaho becomes a state on July 3
    $6÷6=$ $1+7=$ $7+2=$ $9x0=$

8. Former governor Frank Steunenberg is murdered
    $6-5=$ $5+4=$ $2x0=$ $5+0=$

9. First paved highway connecting northern and southern Idaho opens
    $4÷4=$ $3+6=$ $5-2=$ $2+6=$

10. Columbia-Snake River Inland Waterway opens, Lewiston becomes the farthest inland seaport in the West
    $7÷7=$ $3x3=$ $8-1=$ $5x1=$

ANSWERS: 1-1805; 2-1809; 3-1834; 4-1860; 5-1863; 6-1884; 7-1890; 8-1905; 9-1938; 10-1975

What Did We Do Before Money?

In early Idaho, there were no banks. However, people still wanted to barter, trade, or otherwise "purchase" goods from each other. Wampum, made of shells, bone, or stones, was often swapped for goods. Indians, especially, used wampum for "money." In the barter system, people swapped goods or services.

Fur trappers and traders were the first people to settle in Idaho. They traded guns, knives, pots, and mirrors for beaver pelts. Fur trappers, known as mountain men, fur traders, and Native Americans met once a year to trade goods at a gathering called a *rendezvous*.

Later, banks came into existence, and people began to use money to buy goods. However, they also still bartered when they had no money to spend.

Place a star in the box below the systems used today.

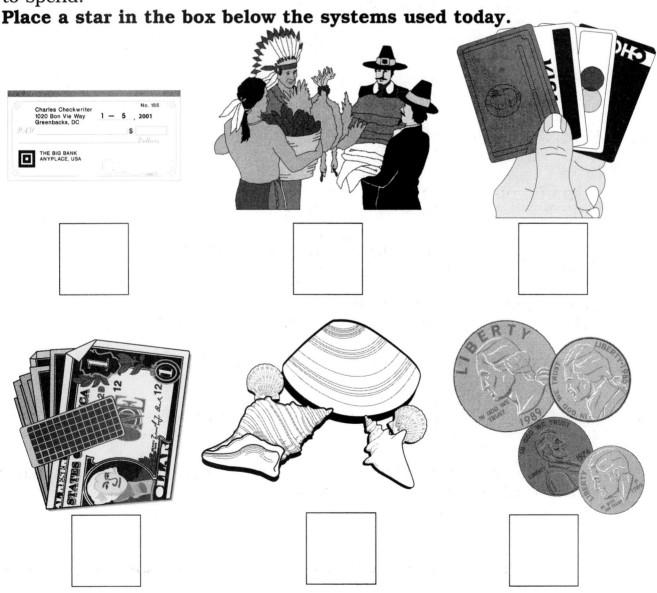

Rhymin' Riddles

1. We lived in Idaho before the explorers did roam;
   On lands near rivers and lakes were our tribes' home.

   Who are we? _____

2. In Idaho I was born, but another tribe took me away;
   I traveled with Lewis and Clark, telling them what the Indians did say.

   Who am I? _____

3. To stop labor unrest, U.S. troops I did call;
   When I opened my front gate, a bomb took away my all.

   Who am I? _____

4. I was known as a mountain man, explorer, and hunter;
   In Idaho I explored the regions of Lemhi, Teton, Cache, Boise, Payette, and Weiser.

   Who am I? _____

Map Symbols

Make up symbols for these names and draw them in the space provided on the right.

cattle	
potatoes	
manufacturing	
gold	
silver	
airport	
sheep	
fort	
railroad	

Idaho Goodies!

Match the name of each crop or product from Idaho with the picture of that item.

Most of Idaho's farms are in the valleys of the Snake River and its tributaries.

Potatoes and wheat are Idaho's main crops.

potatoes

wheat

sugar beets

dry beans

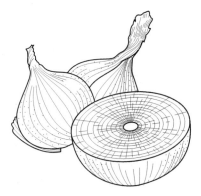

onions

sweet corn

Cattle and sheep ranches are found in Idaho's mountains and drier areas.

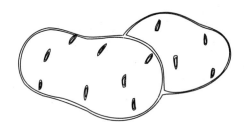

Historical Idaho Women World Wonders!

Idaho has been the home of many brave and influential women. See if you can match these women with their accomplishments.

1. Emma Edwards Green ___
2. Mary Awkright Hutton ___
3. Lana Turner ___
4. Eliza Spalding ___
5. Laura Starcher ___
6. Susan McBeth ___
7. Gracie Bowers Pfost ___
8. Minnie Howard ___
9. Picabo Street ___
10. Margaret Roberts ___

A. came to Idaho with her missionary husband and drew pictures to teach Nez Perce children about the Bible

B. talked 40 Ohio coal miners into going with her to north Idaho's gold mines and was the first woman in history elected as a delegate to the Democratic national convention

C. Olympic skier

D. actress; films included *The Postman Always Rings Twice* and *We Who Are Young*

E. first woman mayor in the United States in 1898

F. designed Idaho's state seal; only woman to design a state seal

G. first Idaho woman to serve as U.S. representative

H. she served as a missionary teacher, along with her sister Kate, to the Nez Perce and compiled a Nez Perce dictionary

I. established Idaho's first free kindergarten; known as the "Susan B. Anthony of Idaho"

J. teacher, doctor; founder of the Pocatello Carnegie Library

ANSWERS: 1-F; 2-B; 3-D; 4-A; 5-E; 6-H; 7-G; 8-J; 9-C; 10-I

Producers and Consumers

Producers (sellers) make goods or provide services. Ralph, a fourth grade student in Ovid is a consumer because he wants to buy a new wheel for his bicycle. Other products and services from Idaho that consumers can buy include electrical equipment, wood products, mining and farming equipment, and food production.

Manufacturers in Idaho build mobile homes and pre-fabricated houses.

Electrical components made in Idaho include computers, peripheral equipment, and semiconductors.

Complete these sentences.

Without **paper**, I couldn't

_____

_____

Without **railroad ties**, I couldn't

_____

_____

Without **furniture**, I couldn't

_____

_____

Without **frozen French fries**, I couldn't

_____

_____

Quick-freezing and dehydrating accounts for nearly half of Idaho's potato production.

Wood products manufactured in Idaho include paper, plywood, veneers, poles, furniture, boxes, and railroad ties.

Idaho Word Wheel!

Use the Word Wheel of Idaho names to complete the sentences below.

1. Philo _____ Farnsworth is known as the "father of television."

2. William Edgar _____ served Idaho as a U.S. senator.

3. Professional baseball player _____ Killebrew led the Minnesota Twins to three championships.

4. _____ Plummer led the outlaw gang known as the Innocents.

5. Henry _____ founded the Lapwai Mission.

6. Elias _____ discovered gold in the Clearwater region in 1860.

7. _____ "Big Train" Johnson is considered one of the greatest pitchers in baseball history.

8. _____ Laird Shoup was the first governor of Idaho.

9. Explorer John _____ was a member of the Lewis and Clark Corps of Discovery.

10. Chief _____ of the Nez Perce led his people on a retreat to Canada before surrendering to U.S. soldiers.

A Plethora of Parks!

Idaho has many state parks, national forests, and national monuments that celebrate its beauty and history! Let's plan a trip through the state and see which direction we need to go to get from park to park.

1. Your trip through Idaho starts on the Idaho-Wyoming border at Yellowstone National Park. Your next stop is Henry's Lake State Park in the Targhee National Forest. **Which way do you go?**

   _____

2. From Henry's Lake, you want to go City of Rocks National Reserve near Almo. **Which direction is it?**

   _____

3. From Almo, you want to go to Hagerman Fossil Beds National Monument near Hagerman. **Which way do you drive?**

   _____

4. John Packer's Cabin State Park near Meadows is your next stop after Hagerman Fossil Beds National Monument. **Which way is it?**

   _____

5. Your final stop on your tour of parks is Priest Lake State Park in the northern tip of the Idaho panhandle. **How do you get there from Meadows?**

   _____

Create Your Own Idaho State Quarter!

Look at the change in your pocket. You might notice that one of the coins has changed. The United States is minting new quarters, one for each of the 50 states. Each quarter has a design on it that says something special about one particular state. The Idaho quarter will be in cash registers and piggy banks everywhere after it's released in 2007.

What if you had designed the Idaho quarter? Draw a picture of how you would like the Idaho quarter to look. Make sure you include things that are special about Idaho.

Idaho Law Comes In Many Flavors!

For each of these people, write down the kind(s) of law used to decide whether their actions are legal or illegal.

1. Bank robber _____

2. Business person _____

3. State park ranger _____

4. Idahoans _____

5. Doctor _____

6. Real estate agent _____

7. Corporate president _____

8. Ship owner _____

9. Diplomat _____

10. Soldier _____

Medical Law

International Law

Military Law

Commercial Law

Maritime Law

Antitrust Law

Criminal Law

State Law

Environmental Law

Property Law

ANSWERS: (Answers may vary.) 1-Criminal; 2-Commercial; 3-Environmental; 4-State; 5-Medical; 6-Property; 7-Antitrust; 8-Maritime; 9-International; 10-Military

Mixed-Up States!

Color, cut out, and paste each of Idaho's six neighbors onto the map below.

Be sure and match the state shapes!

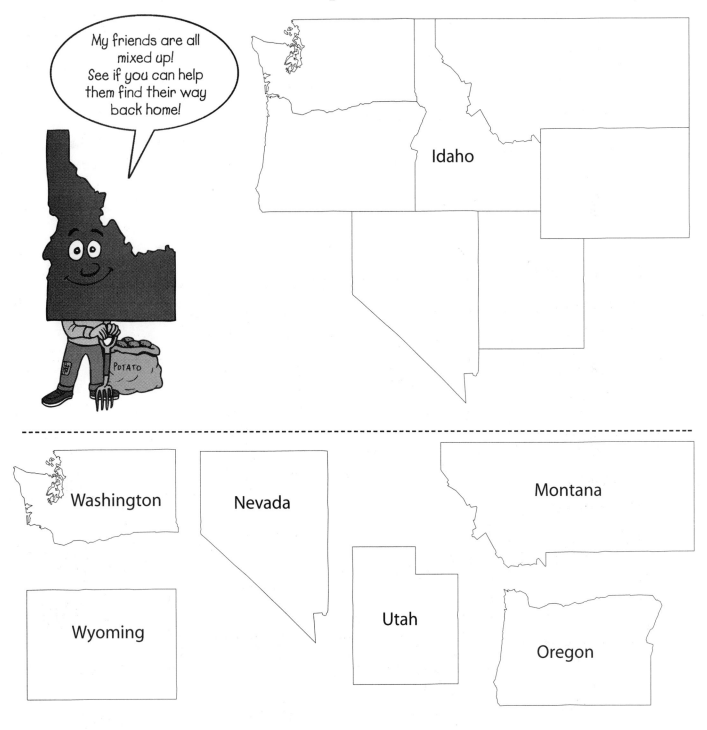

The Port of Lewiston

Not only is Lewiston the only seaport in Idaho, it is the farthest inland port on the west coast! Lewiston became a seaport in 1975 when the Columbia-Snake Inland Waterway was completed. The port is located at the confluence (the coming together of two rivers) of the Snake and Clearwater rivers and is the last stop on the Columbia-Snake Inland Waterway.

The Columbia-Snake Inland Waterway is the second largest water transportation highway in the United States, second only to the Mississippi River.

Barges on the Columbia-Snake Inland Waterway go through a series of eight dams and locks on the waterway to reach the port of Portland, Oregon—465 miles (748 kilometers) away.

When you're on board any kind of boat, you have to use special terms to talk about directions. Label the ship below with these terms:

bow: front of the ship
stern: back of the ship
fore: towards the bow
aft: towards the stern
port: left as you face the bow
starboard: right as you face the bow

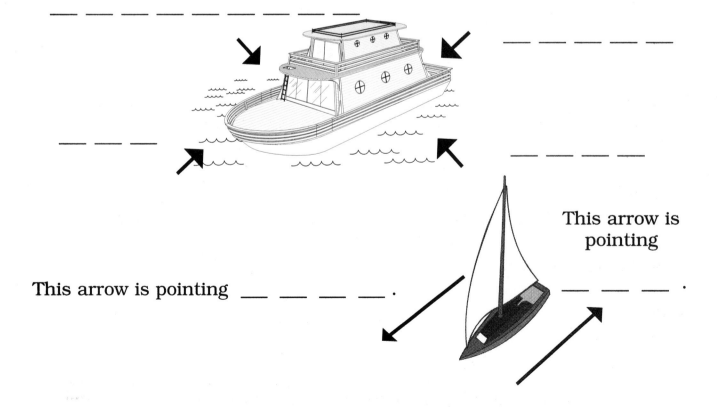

_ _ _ _ _ _ _

_ _ _ _ _

_ _ _ _

_ _ _ _ _

This arrow is pointing

This arrow is pointing _ _ _ _ .

_ _ _ .

Idaho Politics As Usual!

Our elected government officials decide how much money is going to be spent on schools, roads, public parks, and libraries. Every election is important, and everyone who is eligible (able) to vote should do so!

Today, many elected government officials are women. However, before the 19th Amendment to the U.S. Constitution, women were unable to vote in national elections! Women in Idaho were given the right to vote in the state in 1896. As a result, women began running for office, and winning. In 1920, enough states ratified the 19th Amendment, and it became the law of the land. Women gained total suffrage nationally and continue to be a major force in the election process today.

On the lines provided, write down a question for each of the answers below. A hint follows each answer.

1. Question: _____

    Answer: A draft of a law presented for review.

    (Short for William!)

2. Question: _____

    Answer: The right to vote.

    (Don't make us suffer!)

3. Question: _____

    Answer: The ability to forbid a bill or law from being passed.

    (Just say no!)

4. Question: _____

    Answer: The fundamental law of the United States that was framed in 1787 and put into effect in 1789.

    (Idaho has one too!)

5. Question: _____

    Answer: An amendment.

    (It's not something subtracted from #4!)

ANSWERS: (may vary slightly) 1-What is a bill? 2-What is suffrage? 3-What is a veto? 4-What is the Constitution? 5-What is an addition to the Constitution called?

What Shall I Be When I Grow Up?

Here are just a few of the jobs that kept early Idahoans busy.

Lawyer	Carpenter	Baker
Tenant Farmer	Weaver	Pharmacist
Woodcarver	Barber	Gaoler (jailer)
Judge	Gardener	Fisherman
Housekeeper	Printer	Doctor
Silversmith	Cook	Governor
Politician	Musician	Milliner (hatmaker)
Dairyman	Bookbinder	Soldier
Wheelwright	Laundress	Hunter
Teacher	Jeweler	Blacksmith
Servant	Innkeeper	Sailor
Cabinetmaker	Stablehand	Beekeeper
Mayor	Tailor	Gunsmith
Cooper (barrelmaker)	Minister	Prospector

You are a young pioneer trying to decide what you want to be when you grow up.

Choose a career and next to it write a description of what you think you would do each day as a:

Write your career choice here!

_____

Write your career choice here!

_____

Write your career choice here!

_____

Write your career choice here!

_____

Idaho's Governor!

The governor is the leader of the state.

You've been assigned to write a biography of the governor of Idaho.

Before you can start your book, you need to jot down some notes in your trusty computer. Fill in the necessary information in the spaces provided on the dossier!

GOVERNOR'S NAME:

_____

_____

Date of Birth: _____
Place of Birth: _____
Father: _____
Mother: _____
Siblings: _____

Spouse: _____
Children: _____

Pets: _____

Schools Attended: _____
_____

Previous Occupation(s): _____
_____

Likes: _____
_____

Dislikes: _____
_____

abc • APPLICATIONS   MENU   CALCULATOR   FIND   123 •

The ORIGINAL Idaho Natives!

Several early Indian groups made Idaho their home. The Kootenai, Pend d'Oreille, and Coeur d'Alene groups lived in northern Idaho. The Nez Perce settled in the region between Oregon's Blue Mountains and northern Idaho's Bitterroot Mountains. In the summer, the northern Indians ate fish and berries. In the winter, they traveled to Montana to hunt bison, elk, and bear.

The Shoshone, Bannock, and Paiute tribes lived in southern Idaho. They used weirs (an enclosure set in a river to catch fish) and caught salmon by the thousands. Then, they dried and smoked the salmon on wooden racks. They stored the dried meats in pits lined with grass and leaves during the winter.

What kinds of things did Native Americans use in their everyday life? For each of the things shown, circle YES if Native Americans did use it, or NO if they didn't.

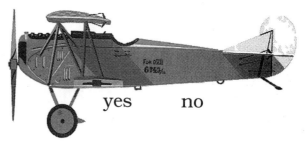

yes   no

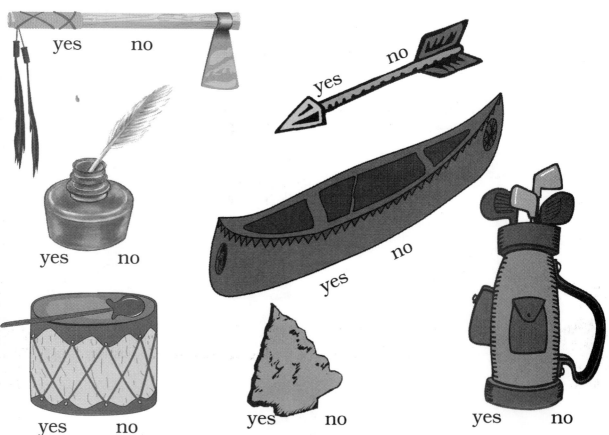

yes   no

yes   no

yes   no

yes   no

yes   no

yes   no

yes   no

Idaho States All Around Code Buster!

USE THIS CODE!!!

Decipher the code and write in the names of the states that border Idaho.

A B C D E F G H I J K L M N O P Q R

S T U V W X Y Z

1. __ __ __ __ __ __ __ __ __ __

2. __ __ __ __ __ __

3. __ __ __ __ __ __ __

4. __ __ __ __ __ __ __

5. __ __ __ __ __ __

6. __ __ __ __

Unique Idaho Place Names!

Can you figure out the compound words that make up the names of these Idaho places?

Ashton _____ _____

Blackfoot _____ _____

Carmen _____ _____

Clearwater _____ _____

Cottonwood _____ _____

Fairfield _____ _____

Fernview _____ _____

Headquarters _____ _____

Lowman _____ _____

Oxford _____ _____

Porthill _____ _____

Potlatch _____ _____

Rockland _____ _____

Sandpoint _____ _____

Southwick _____ _____

Looking For a Home in the Gem State

Can you figure out where these things, people, and animals belong? Use the clues to help you!

1. Lake Pend Oreille covers 148 square miles (383 square kilometers) in Idaho's ⊶—◉ + 🖐 + le.

2. Fish farms on the middle River produce rainbow trout, catfish, and tilapia.

3. Canyons in the Owyhee Plateau are home to (opposite of small) + 🟫 🧍 + ep.

4. Idaho's forests are home to short + 🐾 + ed (short for Robert) "_ _ _" + 🐱 + s

5. 🐰 + 🖌 is a plant found in southern Idaho's deserts.

6. The 🎺 + er 🦢 can be found in the Henry's Fork and Yellowstone areas.

I Love Idaho, Weather or Not!

The mountain ranges around Idaho determine its weather. Moist Pacific air comes in from Washington and Oregon, but most of the rain falls before it gets to Idaho. The mountains along the border with Montana and Wyoming protect Idaho from the Arctic cold those states feel in the winter.

Idaho's temperatures can drop to 16°F (-8.9°C) in the winter and can reach 90°F (32.2°C) in the summer. Orofino holds the record for Idaho's record high temperature at 118°F (48°C), on July 28, 1934. The lowest temperature, -60°F (-51°C), was on January 18, 1943, at Island Park Dam,

FAST FACTS

The Snake River plain receives less than 10 inches (25 centimeters) of rain each year, while northern and central Idaho gets 50 inches (127 centimeters).

Idaho's high mountains can get 200 inches (508 centimeters) of snow in the winter. Northern Idaho gets about 32 inches (81 centimeters) of rain and snow each year.

On the thermometer gauges below, color the mercury red (°F) to show the hottest temperature ever recorded in Idaho. Color the mercury blue (°F) to show the coldest temperature ever recorded in Idaho.

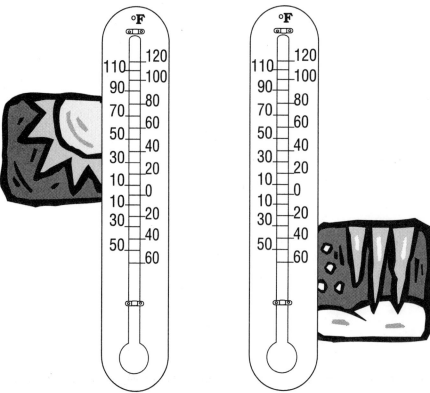

The Scenic Route

Imagine that you've planned an exciting exploratory expedition around Idaho for your classmates. You've chosen some cities and other places to take your friends.

Circle these sites and cities on the map below, then number them in the order you would visit if you were traveling north to south through the state:

_____ Elk River

_____ Naples

_____ Riddle

_____ Smith's Ferry

_____ Bruneau

_____ Placerville

_____ Lake Fork

_____ Coeur d'Alene

Key to a Map!

A map key, also called a map legend, shows symbols which represent different things on a map.

Match each word with a symbol for things found in the state of Idaho.

airport **Boise City Airport**

church **Old Mission of the Sacred Heart, Cataldo**

mountains **Borah Peak**

river **Snake River**

road **I-84, I-15, I-90, I-86**

school **University of Idaho, Moscow**

state capital **Boise**

battle site **Battle of White Bird Canyon, near Grangeville**

bird sanctuary **Snake River Birds of Prey National Conservation Area**

BROTHER, CAN YOU SPARE A DIME?

After the collapse of the stock market on Wall Street in 1929, the state of Idaho, along with the rest of the nation, plunged headfirst into the Great Depression. It was the worst economic crisis America had ever known. Banks closed and businesses crashed...there was financial ruin everywhere.

Idahoans had already had a tough time in the 1920s. Many Idaho farmers had increased production to meet the demands of World War I. Farmers had borrowed money from banks to meet the demand for produce during the war. When the war was over, prices dropped and farmers couldn't make enough money to pay their debts. When the Depression hit, Idaho's economy collapsed!

Our President Helps

While the nation was in the midst of the Depression, Franklin Delano Roosevelt became president. With America on the brink of economic devastation, the federal government stepped forward and hired unemployed people to build parks, bridges, and roads. With this help, and other government assistance, the country began to slowly, and painfully, pull out of the Great Depression. Within the first 100 days of his office, Roosevelt enacted a number of policies to help minimize the suffering of the nation's many unemployed workers. These programs were known as the NEW DEAL. The jobs helped families support themselves and improved the country's infrastructure.

President Franklin D. Roosevelt's New Deal programs put unemployed Idahoans back to work. New Deal programs brought electricity to rural Idaho and built schools, libraries, and roads. The government provided loans to help Idaho's farmers make it through the Depression.

Put an X next to the jobs that were part of Roosevelt's New Deal.

1. computer programmer _____

2. bridge builder _____

3. fashion model _____

4. park builder _____

5. interior designer _____

6. hospital builder _____

7. school builder _____

8. website designer _____

ANSWERS: 2 4 6 7

Idaho Newcomers!

People have come to Idaho from other states and many other countries on almost every continent! As time goes by, Idaho's population grows more diverse. This means that people of different races and from different cultures and ethnic backgrounds have moved to Idaho.

In the past, many immigrants have come to Idaho from Finland, Sweden, Italy, China, and Spain. Idaho is home to the largest concentration of Basques in the United States. Basques are descendants of people from northern Spain. The largest colony in the world outside of Spain's Pyrenees Mountains lives in Idaho. Idaho's gold rush brought Chinese immigrants to the area to work in mines. When the gold rush was over, they stayed and opened businesses and farmed.

More recently, people have migrated to Idaho from Hispanic countries such as Mexico. Only a certain number of immigrants are allowed to move to America each year. Many of these immigrants eventually become U.S. citizens.

Read the statement and decide if it's a fact or an opinion. Write your answer on the line.

1. Many of Idaho's early immigrants came from Europe. _____

2. Lots of immigrants speak a language other than English. _____

3. The clothing immigrants wear is very interesting. _____

4. Immigrants from Spain have a neat accent when they speak. _____

5. Many immigrants will become United States citizens. _____

6. People have immigrated to Idaho from nearly every country in the world. _____

An immigrant is a person who migrates to another country in hopes of a better life.

ANSWERS: 1-fact; 2-fact; 3-opinion; 4-opinion; 5-fact; 6-fact

A Day in the Life of an Idaho Pioneer

Pretend you are a pioneer in the days of early Idaho. You keep a diary of what you do each day. Write in the "diary" what you might have done on a long, hot summer day in July 1860.

_____

_____

_____

_____

_____

_____

_____

_____

_____

_____

_____

_____

_____

_____

This Old House!

Take yourself back 100 years. Can you imagine what life would be like in the Victorian Era? What did turn-of-the-century Idahoans own? How did they live?

See if you can pick out which of the following items people at the turn of the century had and which ones they did not.

Circle the things you might find or use around your 1900 home.

Home, Sweet Home!

Idaho has been the home of many different authors. Here are just a few. See if you can locate their hometowns on the map of Idaho below! Write the number of each author near the town where he or she lived. Some towns may be used twice.

1. **Carol Ryrie Brink** is from a town close to the Washington border, west of Troy and the home of the University of Idaho. She received a Newbery Award in 1936 for *Caddie Woodlawn*.

2. **Vardis Fisher** was born in a town on the Snake River east of Menan and north of Rigby. He wrote about frontier Idaho in his novels. His works include *A Tale of Valor*, *The Children of God*, and *Mountain Man*.

3. **Ernest Hemingway** spent his last few years near this town north of Hailey in the Sawtooth National Forest. He is best known for *The Old Man and the Sea*, *For Whom the Bell Tolls*, and *A Farewell to Arms*.

4. **W. Wilson Rawls** lived in this city located south of Lewisville on the Snake River for almost 20 years. He wrote *Where the Red Fern Grows* while living in Idaho.

5. **James H. Hawley** was a lawyer and politician. He served as mayor of Idaho's capital city, which is located on the Snake River below Star and Eagle. He wrote *History of Idaho* and *Gem of the Mountains*.

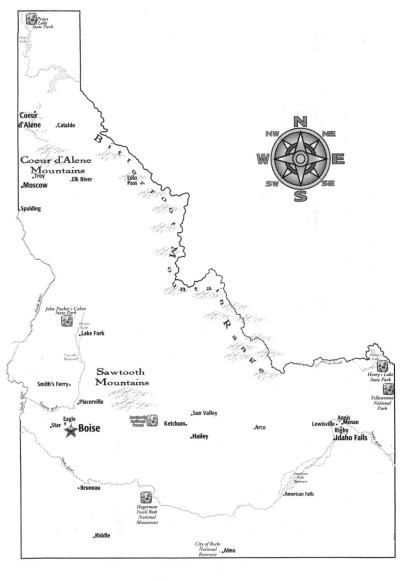

ANSWERS: 1-Moscow; 2-Annis; 3-Ketchum; 4-Idaho Falls, 5-Boise

Idaho Spelling Bee!

Good spelling is a good habit. Study the words on the left side of the page. Then fold the page in half and "take a spelling test" on the right side. Have a buddy read the words aloud to you. When finished, unfold the page and check your spelling. Keep your score. GOOD LUCK.

Each word is worth 5 points.

A perfect score is 100! How many did you get right?

Appaloosa _____

Boise _____

canyon _____

Coeur d'Alene _____

environment _____

evergreen _____

government _____

hydroelectric _____

Kutenai _____

literature _____

mountains _____

nuclear _____

Pend Oreille _____

petroglyph _____

pioneer _____

potato _____

Shoshone _____

skiing _____

volcanoes _____

wilderness _____

Naturally Idaho!

Fill in the bubblegram with some Idaho crops and natural resources. Use the letter clues to help you.

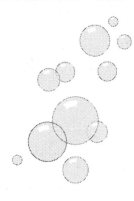
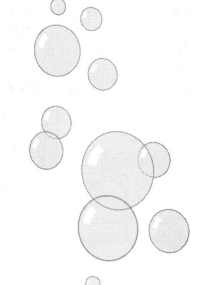

WORD BANK
barley
beef cattle
cherries
mint
onions
phosphate rock
potatoes
silver
sugar beets

1. p 〇 __ a __ 〇 __ s

2. s __ l 〇 __ __

3. o 〇 __ o 〇 __

4. p h __ __ __ h __ 〇 __ r __ __ c __

5. b __ __ f __ 〇 __ t __ __ __

6. b __ __ l 〇 __ __

7. 〇 h __ r 〇 i __ __

8. m 〇 n __

9. 〇 __ g __ __ b __ __ t __

Now unscramble the "bubble" letters to find out the mystery word! HINT: What is one way we can help to save our environment?

__ __ __ __ __ __ __ __ __ __ __ __

MYSTERY WORD: conservation
ANSWERS: 1-potatoes; 2-silver; 3-onions; 4-phosphate rock; 5-beef cattle; 6-barley; 7-cherries; 8-mint; 9-sugar beets

Mining in Idaho!

With a nickname like the Gem State, it's no surprise that more than 80 kinds of gemstones are found in Idaho. The star garnet is the state's official gemstone. Mines in Idaho produce 13,000 tons (11,793 metric tons) of garnet sand used as an abrasive by industrial users, as well as for gems. Minerals used in the construction industry are mined in Idaho and include perlite, crushed stone, sand, gravel, and pumice. Idaho is one of the U.S. leaders in the mining of lead and zinc. Other minerals found in Idaho include phosphate rock, cadmium, tungsten, vanadium, and molybdenum. Silver and gold brought prospectors to Idaho in the 1860s, and silver and gold are still found in Idaho. Idaho remains a leading producer of silver.

Put these items in alphabetical order from 1-10.

_____ star garnet

_____ gold

_____ silver

_____ phosphate rock

_____ lead

_____ zinc

_____ cadmium

_____ tungsten

_____ vanadium

_____ molybdenum

What a Great Idea!

WORD BANK

Arco	Grigg
grocery	Simplot
ski lift	television

1. Brothers Nephi and Golden __ __ __ __ __ tried quick-freezing potatoes, the beginning of frozen French fries, and developed the shredded potato treat known as Tater Tots™.

2. Idaho businessman J.R. __ __ __ __ __ __ __ , known as "Mr. Spud," has been named as the "richest man in Idaho" by *Fortune* magazine.

3. Philo T. Farnsworth, who went to high school in Rigby, produced the first all-electronic __ __ __ __ __ __ __ __ __ __ image and holds patents on the cathode ray tube and more than 300 other inventions.

4. Joe Albertson of Caldwell founded the __ __ __ __ __ __ __ chain known, as Albertson's, one of the largest in the United States.

5. __ __ __ __, Idaho, was the first town in the world to be completely powered by nuclear energy for one hour on July 17, 1955.

6. Union Pacific Railroad engineers built the world's first __ __ __ __ __ __ __ at Sun Valley, Idaho's best-known ski resort.

Famous Idahoan Scavenger Hunt!

Here is a list of some of the famous people associated with our state. **Go on a scavenger hunt to see if you can "capture" a fact about each one. Use an encyclopedia, almanac, or other resource you might need. Happy hunting!**

Moses Alexander _____

Cecil Andrus _____

Ezra Taft Benson _____

William Edgar Borah _____

Gutzon Borglum _____

Chief Joseph _____

Frank R. Church _____

Gretchen Fraser _____

Joseph Garry _____

William "Big Bill" Haywood _____

Harmon Killebrew _____

Mariel Hemingway _____

Jerry Kramer _____

Dan O'Brien _____

Ezra Pound _____

Sacajawea _____

George Laird Shoup _____

Picabo Street _____

Jackson Sundown _____

Lana Turner _____

One Day, One Night!

Use the words from the Word Bank to fill in the blanks in the story below. Some words may be used more than once.

WORD BANK

bear

chipmunk

council

coyote

salmon

According to Nez Percé legend, a great __ __ __ __ __ __ __ was held in the days of the animal kingdom to help them get ready for the coming of mankind.

The __ __ __ __ __ __, the animals' leader, and the council made decisions on how long winter should last, when the __ __ __ __ __ __ should come up the river, and where animals should live.

The last question was how to divide night from day. The grizzly __ __ __ __ wanted five years of day and five years of night, enough time to get in a good sleep. The __ __ __ __ __ __ __ __ said little animals couldn't last that long without food.

They argued until the __ __ __ __ became confused and agreed with the __ __ __ __ __ __ __ __ —one day, one night! The bear became so angry he scratched stripes down chipmunk's back.

The __ __ __ __ __ __ felt sorry for the bear. He told bear to find a cave in the mountains and sleep during the long winter months.

Map of North America

This is a map of North America. Idaho is one of the 50 states.

Color the state of Idaho red.

Color the rest of the United States yellow. Alaska and Hawaii are part of the United States and should also be colored yellow.

Color Canada green. Color Mexico blue.

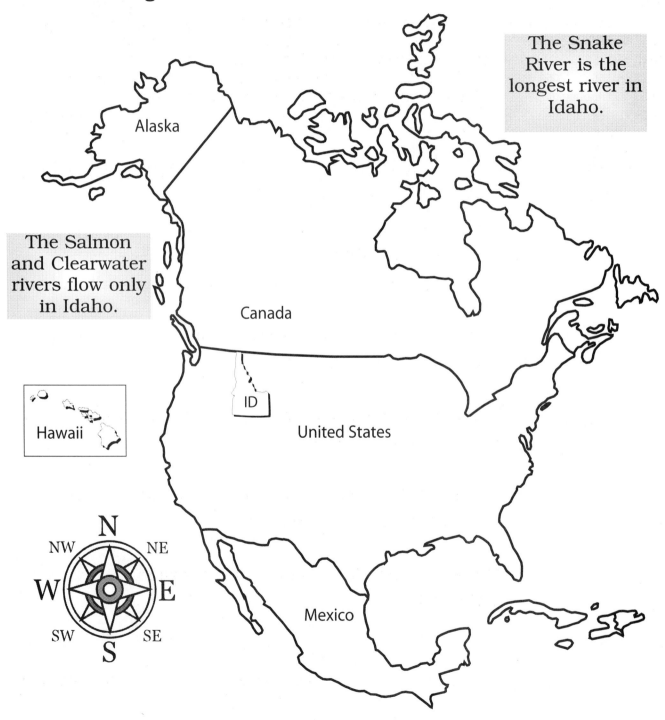

The Snake River is the longest river in Idaho.

Alaska

The Salmon and Clearwater rivers flow only in Idaho.

Canada

ID

Hawaii

United States

N
NW   NE
W   E
SW   SE
S

Mexico

Craters of the Moon!

True or False?!

Craters of the Moon National Monument got its name because the area looks like the surface of the moon does through a telescope! In fact, astronauts have trained in the area for that reason.

The 83 square-mile (215 square-kilometer) area, located southwest of Arco, was created by volcanic eruptions and lava flows that started 15,000 years ago and ended about 2,000 years ago. The area's features include volcanic cinder cones, lava flows, craters, and caves. The area was proclaimed a national monument by President Calvin Coolidge in 1924.

Read each sentence, and decide if it is TRUE or FALSE. Write your answers on the lines provided.

_____ 1. Craters of the Moon got its name because it looks like the surface of a planet.

_____ 2. Craters of the Moon was created by volcanic eruptions and lava flows.

_____ 3. President Herbert Hoover declared the area a national monument in 1924.

_____ 4. Craters of the Moon is an area of 83 square miles (215 square kilometers).

_____ 5. Craters of the Moon is located southwest of Twin Falls.

ANSWERS: 1-FALSE; 2-TRUE; 3-FALSE; 4-TRUE; 5-FALSE

Idaho State Greats!

In the paragraph about important people from Idaho below there are eight misspelled words. Circle the misspelled words, and then spell them correctly on the lines provided.

Joseph Garry served as tribal liter of the Coeur d'Alene for 20 years. He also served as president of the National Congres of American Indians, the largest Native American group in the Uknighted States. Chief Joseph of the Nez Perce refused to sign a treatie that striped his people of their land, then lead them on a 1,800-mile (2,900-kilometer) retreat to Canada before surrendering to U.S. soldiers. Tendoy was cheef of the Lemhi band of the Shoshone who erned the respect of both his people and the U.S. government. He opposed his tribe's relocation to a reservation.

_____   _____

_____   _____

_____   _____

ANSWERS: 1-leader; 2-Congress; 3-United; 4-treaty; 5-stripped; 6-led; 7-chief; 8-earned

Virtual Idaho!

It's time to build your own website! We've given you pictures of things that have to do with Idaho. Color and cut them out, and arrange them on a blank piece of paper to create a web page that will make people want to visit Idaho!

Tarzan of the Apes!

Edgar Rice Burroughs, the creator of Tarzan, has Idaho ties. He owned a stationary store in Pocatello and also worked with an Idaho mining company after serving in the military. He wrote the first draft of Tarzan while living in Idaho. He published his first Tarzan novel, *Tarzan of the Apes*, in 1912. Since then, there have been 26 Tarzan novels and more than 43 Tarzan movies, as well as magazine stories, comic books, and television programs.

In Burroughs' books, Tarzan is John Clayton, Lord Greystoke. He was orphaned as a child and raised by an ape. He became leader of the apes and was known unofficially as "king of the jungle." Tarzan became immortal because of an African shaman's (holy man's) secret formula. Tarzan learned to read after finding the remains of a book in his parents' hut on the west coast of Africa. He married an American woman named Jane Porter.

Read each sentence, and decide if it is FACT or FICTION. Write your answers on the lines provided.

_____ 1. Tarzan was "king of the jungle."

_____ 2. Edgar Rice Burroughs created Tarzan.

_____ 3. Burroughs lived in Idaho.

_____ 4. Tarzan was immortal.

_____ 5. Tarzan's real name was John Clayton, Lord Greystoke.

ANSWERS: 1-FICTION, 2-FACT, 3-FACT, 4-FICTION, 5-FICTION

A River Runs Through It!

The state of Idaho is blessed with many rivers. See if you can wade right in and figure out these rivers' names! **For each river code, circle every other letter (beginning with the second one) to discover the name!**

RIVER BANK
Coeur d'Alene   Bear   Clearwater   Little Lost   Salmon   Snake

1. A river that "slithers" through Idaho and forms the state's border with Oregon

   X S B N M A J K L E

2. A river that is "small" and disappears in Butte County

   W L R I D T U T O L H E   F L F O K S L T

3. This river, named after a fish, flows only in Idaho

   R S B A V L S M Z O K N

4. River that shares its name with animals that are black, brown, polar, panda, or grizzly

   Y B O E F A C R

5. Name of the river that is not cloudy and has water in its name

   A C S L V E M A N R J W G A H T F E Y R

6. River that shares its name with an Idaho Native American tribe and city

   O C P O L E J U M R   B D V A X L Z E S N G E

Idaho Firsts!

First Nuclear Power Plant!
The first power plant in the world to produce electricity by using nuclear energy was Experimental Breeder Reactor #1, near Arco, on December 20, 1951.

First City to Get Nuked!
The first city to have power provided completely by nuclear energy for one hour was Arco on July 17, 1955.

Woman Designs the State Seal!
The first, and only, state seal designed by a woman was Idaho's. Emma Edwards Green created the state seal in 1890.

First School!
The first school in Idaho opened in 1837 at the Lapwai Mission.

First Ski Lift!
Union Pacific Railroad engineers built the world's first ski lift at Sun Valley, Idaho's best-known ski resort.

First Church Service!
The Methodist Episcopal Church held the first church service in Idaho in 1834 in Fort Hall.

Which of these "firsts" happened first?

____ Emma Edwards Green designs Idaho state seal

____ First power plant to produce electricity by using nuclear energy

____ First school opens

ANSWER: First school opens

Idaho Gazetteer

A gazetteer is a list of places. For each of these famous Idaho places, write down the town in which it's located, and one interesting fact about the place. You may have to use an encyclopedia, almanac, or other resource to find the information, so dig deep!

1. Saint Joseph's Mission _ _ _ _ _ _ _ _ _ _
   _____

2. Idaho State Historical Museum _ _ _ _ _ _
   _____

3. Idaho Museum of Natural History _ _ _ _ _ _ _ _ _
   _____

4. Silent City of Rocks _ _ _ _
   _____

5. Shoshone Ice Cave _ _ _ _ _ _ _ _
   _____

6. Nez Perce National Historical Park _ _ _ _ _ _ _ _
   _____

7. Sierra Silver Mine _ _ _ _ _ _ _
   _____

8. Balanced Rock _ _ _ _ _ _ _ _ _
   _____

WORD BANK

Almo	Boise	Castleford	
Cottonwood	Pocatello	Shoshone	Spalding

Pioneer Corn Husk Doll

You can make a corn husk doll similar to the dolls
Idaho pioneer children played with! Here's how:

You will need:
- corn husks (or strips of cloth)
- string
- scissors

1. **Select a long piece of corn husk and fold
   it in half. Tie a string about one inch
   (2.54 centimeters) down from the fold to
   make the doll's head.**

2. **Roll a husk and put it between the layers of the tied husk,
   next to the string. Tie another string around the longer
   husk, just below the rolled husk. Now your doll has arms!
   Tie short pieces of string at the ends of the rolled husk to
   make the doll's hands.**

3. **Make your doll's waist by tying another string around the
   longer husk.**

4. **If you want your doll to have legs, cut the longer husk up
   the middle. Tie the two halves at the bottom to
   make feet.**

5. **Add eyes and a nose to your doll with a marker. You could
   use corn silk for the doll's hair.**

**Now you can
make a whole
family of dolls!**

Idaho Timeline!

A timeline is a list of important events and the year that they happened. You can use a timeline to understand more about history.

Read the timeline about Idaho history, then see if you can answer the questions at the bottom.

1730	Shoshone Indians acquire horses
1805	Lewis and Clark Corps of Discovery travels through Idaho
1809	The first trading post in the area is built at Lake Pend Oreille by David Thompson
1860	Elias Pierce discovers gold on Orofino Creek
1863	Idaho becomes a U.S. territory
1884	Silver deposits found in Coeur d'Alene Mountains
1890	Idaho becomes a state on July 3
1905	Former governor Frank Steunenberg is murdered
1938	First paved highway connecting northern and southern Idaho opens
1942	Thousands of Japanese-Americans living on the Pacific Coast are sent to Minidoka Relocation Center in Jerome County

Now put yourself back in the proper year if you were the following people.

1. If you are excited because Idaho became a U.S. territory, the year would be _____.

2. If heard about a gold strike in Idaho, the year would be _____.

3. If you were riding on the first paved highway from north Idaho to south Idaho, the year would be _____.

4. If you were with the Lewis and Clark expedition in Idaho, the year would be _____.

5. If you read about the death of former governor Frank Steunenberg in the newspaper, the year would be _____.

6. If you saw a Shoshone Indian on a horse for the first time, the year would be _____.

7. If you were excited because Idaho became a state, the year would be _____.

8. If you brought furs to trade for the first time in Pend d'Oreille, the year would be _____.

ANSWERS: 1-1863; 2-1860; 3-1938; 4-1805; 5-1905; 6-1730; 7-1890; 8-1809

Idaho State Economy!

Idaho banks provide essential financial services.
Some of the services that banks provide include:
- They lend money to consumers to purchase goods and services such as houses, cars, and education.
- They lend money to producers who start new businesses.
- They issue credit cards.
- They provide savings accounts and pay interest to savers.
- They provide checking accounts.

Circle whether you would have more, less, or the same amount of money after each event.

1. You deposit your paycheck into your checking account.   MORE   LESS   SAME

2. You put $1,000 in your savings account.   MORE   LESS   SAME

3. You use your credit card to buy new school clothes.   MORE   LESS   SAME

4. You borrow money from the bank to open a toy store.   MORE   LESS   SAME

5. You write a check at the grocery store.   MORE   LESS   SAME

6. You transfer money from checking to savings.   MORE   LESS   SAME

Tourists spend around $1.8 billion in Idaho each year!

They visit Idaho's mountains, forests, lakes, and waterfalls. each year!

ANSWERS: 1.more 2.more 3.less 4.more 5.less 6.same

I Am A Famous Person From Idaho

From the Word Bank, find my name and fill in the blank.

WORD BANK

Moses Alexander   Jim Bridger
Walter "Big Train" Johnson
William McConnell
Henry Spalding
Edward A. (E.A.) Stevenson

1. I was a mountain man who explored Idaho. I was respected for my storytelling skills and my knowledge of Indians.
   Who am I? _____ _____

2. I served Idaho as governor from 1915-1919. I was the nation's first Jewish governor.
   Who am I? _____ _____

3. I was a missionary. I founded Lapwai Mission.
   Who am I? _____ _____

4. I served Idaho as governor and a U.S. senator. I fought for woman suffrage and irrigation laws.
   Who am I? _____ _____

5. I was governor of Idaho Territory from 1885-1889. I convinced President Grover Cleveland not to divide Idaho into more than one state.
   Who am I? _____ _____

6. I was a professional baseball player and was one of the first five players named to the Baseball Hall of Fame. I struck out 3,508 batters, a record I kept for more than 50 years
   Who am I? _____ _____

ANSWERS: 1-Jim Bridger; 2-Moses Alexander; 3-Henry Spalding; 4-William McConnell; 5-Edward A. (E.A.) Stevenson; 6-Walter "Big Train" Johnson

Weis Rockshelter

Weis Rockshelter is a notch in a cliff in Grave's Creek Canyon. It is named for the amateur archaeologist who found it. Artifacts from the Weis Rockshelter are stored at the University of Idaho. The artifacts have shown that the Nez Perce lived in the area for 8,000 years.

You are an archaeologist digging into one an area near Weis Rockshelter. Below are pictures of some of the artifacts that you find. Now, you have to identify these strange objects and their uses. **Write down what you think these things are for!**

_____

_____

_____

_____

_____

_____

_____

_____

_____

Idaho Native Americans!

When the explorers arrived in Idaho, there were several Native American groups already living there. Several early Indian groups made Idaho their home. The Kootenai, Pend d'Oreille, and Coeur d'Alene groups lived in northern Idaho. The Nez Perce settled in the region between Oregon's Blue Mountains and northern Idaho's Bitterroot Mountains. In the summer, the northern Indians ate fish and berries. In the winter, they traveled to Montana to hunt bison, elk, and bear.

The Shoshone, Bannock, and Paiute tribes lived in southern Idaho. They used weirs (an enclosure set in a river to catch fish) and caught salmon by the thousands. Then, they dried and smoked the salmon on wooden racks. They stored the dried meats in pits lined with grass and leaves during the winter.

Draw a line from each group to its location on the map.

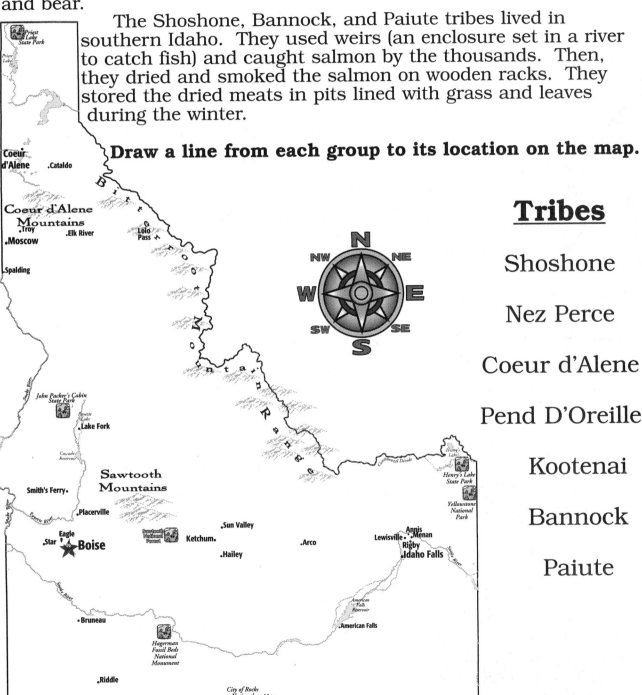

Tribes

Shoshone

Nez Perce

Coeur d'Alene

Pend D'Oreille

Kootenai

Bannock

Paiute

IT'S MONEY IN THE BANK!!

You spent the summer working at **Albertson's**, and you made a lot of money...$500 to be exact! **Solve the math problems below.**

TOTAL EARNED: $500.00

I will pay back my Mom this much
for money I borrowed when I first
started working. Thanks, Mom!   A. $20.00

    subtract A from $500   B. _____

I will give my little brother this much
money for taking my phone messages
while I was at work: C. $10.00

    subtract C from B   D. _____

I will spend this much on a special
treat or reward for myself: E. $25.00

    subtract E from D   F. _____

I will save this much for college: G. $300.00

    subtract G from F   H. _____

I will put this much in my new
savings account so I can buy school   I. $100.00
clothes:

    subtract I from H   J. _____

TOTAL STILL AVAILABLE
             (use answer J)   _____

TOTAL SPENT   (add A, C, and E)   _____

All Eyes Are On Idaho

Find these Idaho city names in the word search:

WORD BANK:

ALBION
ASHTON
BLACKFOOT
CASCADE
CONNOR
DRIGGS
MONTPELIER
NAMPA

OROFINO
PAYETTE
PICABO
PLUMMER
PRESTON
RIGGINS
SANDPOINT

```
B O G B K A T L V Q I W U F H
D E D B M H O A A Z Y S Z G B
O R D A I R O Q Z W H S Q X Z
R M I A E F F P R E S T O N U
O E Z G C X K P A L B I O N T
F A I K G S C N L F A J O N O
I S I L F S A L P U Q E I D B
N H C W E M L C U P M O A D A
O T U L P P B H R H P M P D C
W O R A L R T I Y D R V E P I
V N L V O B G N N P Z N F R P
U R F N E G Z A O A Q X E S Z
U W N V I J S P P M G L N T K
G O J N E T T E Y A P O F M H
C J S E Q Q C C Z V C L D Y C
```

Numbering the Idahoans!

STATE OF IDAHO
CENSUS REPORT

Every ten years, it's time for Idahoans to stand up and be counted. Since 1790, the United States has conducted a census, or count, of each of its citizens. **Practice filling out a pretend census form.**

Name _____ Age [ ]

Place of Birth _____

Current Address _____

Does your family own or rent where you live? _____

How long have you lived in Idaho? _____

How many people are in your family? _____

How many females? [ ] How many males? [ ]

What are their ages? _____

How many rooms are in your house? [ ]

How is your home heated? _____

How many cars does your family own? [ ]

How many telephones are in your home? [ ]

Is your home a farm? _____

Sounds pretty nosy, doesn't it? But a census is very important. The information is used for all kinds of purposes, including setting budgets, zoning land, determining how many schools to build, and much more. The census helps Idaho leaders plan for the future needs of its citizens. Hey, that's you!!

Endangered and Threatened Idaho

Each state has a list of the endangered species found within its borders. An animal is labeled endangered when it is at risk of becoming extinct, or dying out completely. Land development, changes in climate and weather, and changes in the number of predators are all factors that can cause an animal to become extinct. Today many states are passing laws to help save animals on the endangered species list.

Can you help rescue these endangered and threatened animals by filling in their names below?

1. W __ __ D L __ N __   C __ R __ B __ __

2. W H __ __ P __ __ G   C R __ N __

3. S __ __ K __ Y __   S __ L M __ __

4. G R __ __   W __ L __

5. B R __ __ __ __ U   H __ __   S P __ __ __ G __ N __ __ L

6. W __ __ T __   S T __ __ G __ __ N

Circle the animal that is extinct (not here anymore).

Idaho's State Song

"Here We Have Idaho"
Written by McKinley Helm and Albert J. Tompkins
Music by Sallie Hume-Douglas

And here we have Idaho
Winning her way to fame.
Silver and gold in the sunlight blaze,
And romance lies in her name.

Singing, we're singing of you,
Ah, proudly, too; all our lives through,
We'll go singing, singing of you,
Singing of Idaho.

There's truly one state in this great land of ours,
Where ideals can be realized.
The pioneers made it so for you and me,

A legacy we'll always prize.

Answer the following questions:

1. What colors blaze in the sunlight? _____

2. What can be realized in Idaho? _____

3. What lies in Idaho's name? _____

4. What is Idaho winning her way to? _____

ANSWERS: (may vary slightly) 1-silver and gold; 2-ideals; 3-romance; 4-fame

Getting Ready To Vote in Idaho

When you turn 18, you will be eligible to vote. Your vote counts! Many elections have been won by just a few votes. **The following is a form for your personal voting information. You will need to do some research to get all the answers!**

I will be eligible to vote on this date _____

I live in this Congressional District _____

I live in this State Senate District _____

I live in this State Representative District _____

I live in this Voting Precinct _____

The first local election I can vote in will be _____

The first state election I can vote in will be _____

The first national election I can vote in will be _____

The governor of our state is _____

One of my state senators is _____

One of my state representatives is _____

The local public office I would like to run for is _____

The state public office I would like to run for is _____

The federal public office I would like to run for is _____

Did you know that our state government has 35 senators?

The number of legislators may change after each census.

No, but I do know we have 70 representatives!

Idaho State Seal

The state seal features the major industries, forestry and agriculture, and Idaho's beauty. The elk's head above the shield represents the protection of elk and deer. The seal also features the state flower, the Snake River, and state motto.

Color the state seal.

Idaho State Symbol Scramble!

Unscramble the names of these symbols for the state of Idaho. Write the answers in the word wheel around the picture of each symbol.

1. O U T C T A H R T   U R T O T

    Hint: I get my name from the red to orange slash on the underside of my lower jaw.

2. L P S A P A O A O

    Hint: I am known for my spots.

3. R S A T   N A T R G E

    Hint: I get my name from the star that seems to glide or float on my surface.

4. S A E R Q U   E A D C N

    Hint: My steps are a lot of fun when you hear fiddle music.

5. T N R E E S W   E T H I W   N P I E

    Hint: I have soft blue green needles.

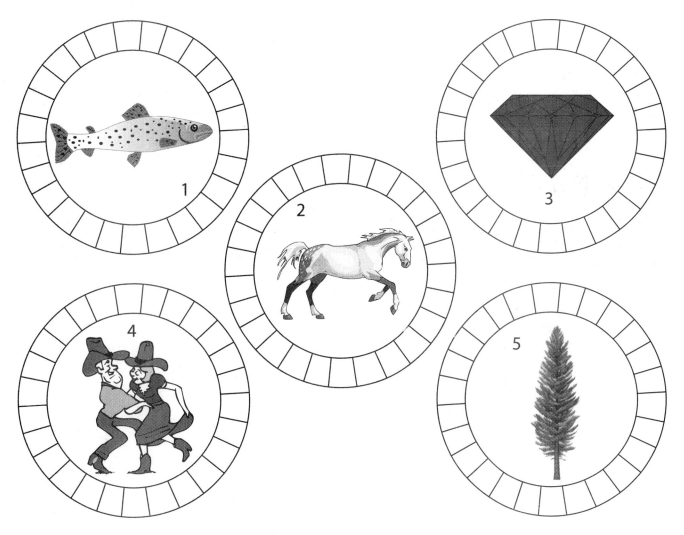

A Quilt Of Many Counties

Idaho has 44 counties. Idaho's counties are political and geographical divisions. Each county elects three county commissioners. The commissioners supervise the county's business affairs. Elected county officials also include the sheriff, assessor, coroner, prosecuting attorney, treasurer, and recorder.

– **Label your county. Color it red.**
– **Label the counties that touch your county. Color them blue.**
– **Now color the rest of the counties green.**

Contributions by Idaho Minorities

Idaho's minority residents have played an important part in the state's history. African-Americans were among the miners, explorers, trappers, soldiers, and cowboys who settled in Idaho in the 1860s. Rhodes Creek is named after miner William Rhodes who made more than $80,000. Blackman Peak in the White Cloud Mountains is named after George Washington Blackman, another miner.

Idaho's gold rush also brought the first Chinese people to Idaho. They worked old worn-out mines that others had left. After the gold rush ended, many of the Chinese stayed and opened businesses. "China Polly" Bemis was a Chinese slave who was smuggled into the United States in the 1870s. The biographical novel *Thousand Pieces of Gold* by Ruthanne Lum McCunn is based on her life. C.K. Ah-Fong was a Chinese doctor who settled near Boise. He earned his medical license from Idaho Territory and specialized in herbal remedies.

Read each statement about these important people and decide whether the statement is a FACT or an OPINION. Write your answer on the line.

_____1. C.K. Ah-Fong's patients liked his herbal remedies.

_____2. "China Polly" Bemis was a Chinese slave.

_____3. William Rhodes made a fortune as a miner.

_____4. *Thousand Pieces of Gold* is a very good book.

_____5. Many of the people who settled Idaho were minorities.

ANSWERS: 1-opinion; 2-fact; 3-fact; 4-opinion; 5-fact

Investigating Idaho's Caves

Idaho has several interesting places for future SPELEOLOGISTS to check out! The most famous underground CAVERNS in Idaho are the Shoshone Ice Caves. The caves have a GLACIER that measures 1,000 feet (305 meters) long and 40 feet (12 meters) high. Idaho pioneers QUARRIED ice from the caves to PRESERVE their food. STALAGMITES come up out of a lake of pure ice in the Crystal Ice Cave. Water from BENEATH the earth's surface dribbles into the cave, then freezes into the cave's unusual ice formations. Minnetonka Cave has walls of crystal ice, nine rooms, and chambers of STALACTITES and stalagmites.

See if you can figure out the meanings of these words from the story above.

1. speleologists:_____

_____

2. caverns:_____

_____

3. glacier:_____

_____

4. quarried:_____

_____

5. preserve:_____

_____

6. stalagmites:_____

_____

7. beneath:_____

_____

8. stalactites:_____

_____

Now check your answers in a dictionary. How close did you get to the real definitions?

Which Founding Person Am I?

From the Word Bank, find my name and fill in the blank.

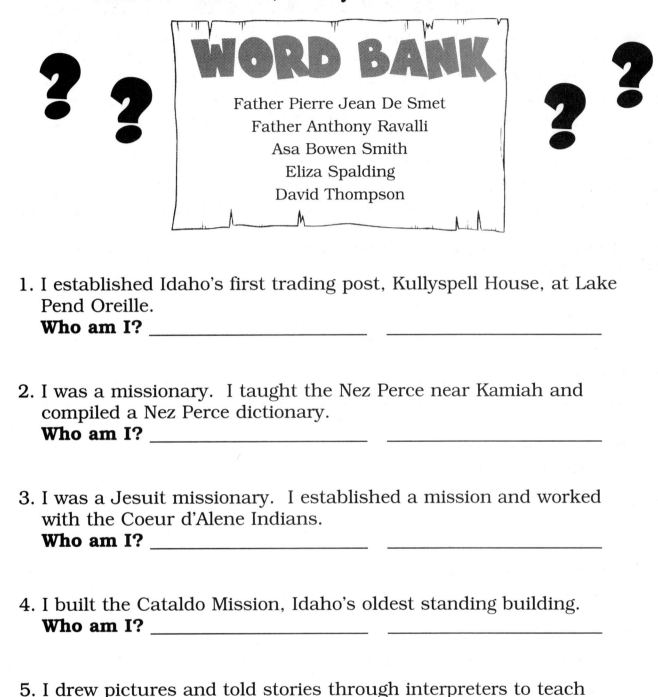

WORD BANK

Father Pierre Jean De Smet

Father Anthony Ravalli

Asa Bowen Smith

Eliza Spalding

David Thompson

1. I established Idaho's first trading post, Kullyspell House, at Lake Pend Oreille.
   Who am I? _____   _____

2. I was a missionary. I taught the Nez Perce near Kamiah and compiled a Nez Perce dictionary.
   Who am I? _____   _____

3. I was a Jesuit missionary. I established a mission and worked with the Coeur d'Alene Indians.
   Who am I? _____   _____

4. I built the Cataldo Mission, Idaho's oldest standing building.
   Who am I? _____   _____

5. I drew pictures and told stories through interpreters to teach Native American children about the Bible.
   Who am I? _____   _____

!! It Could Happen— And It Did! !!

These historical events from Idaho's past are all out of order. Can you put them back together in the correct order? Number these events from 1 to 10, beginning with the earliest.
(There's a great big hint at the end of each sentence.)

___ Former governor Frank Steunenberg is murdered (1905)

___ Idaho becomes a state on July 3 (1890)

___ Members of the Lewis and Clark expedition travel through Idaho (1805)

___ Fort Hall and Fort Boise are established (1834)

___ Idaho becomes a U.S. territory (1863)

___ Columbia-Snake River Inland Waterway opens, Lewiston becomes the farthest inland seaport in the West (1975)

___ Thousands of Japanese Americans living on the Pacific Coast are sent to Minidoka Relocation Center in Jerome County (1942)

___ U.S. soldiers defeat the Nez Perce Indians (1877)

___ Shoshone Indians acquire horses (1730)

___ The United States buys Louisiana Territory, which includes part of present day Idaho, from France (1803)

I Want to be a Cowboy!

The Old West is still alive in Idaho! Many of the settlers who came to Idaho started cattle ranches. Ranching is still important in many parts of the state, and so are the cowboys who work on the ranches. Rodeos are competitions that allow cowboys to show off their skills. Jackson Sundown, a Nez Perce horseman, won the World Saddle Bronc Riding Championship at the age of 50 in 1916 and is the only Native American to win the title. Rodeo events held in Idaho include the Dodge National Finals Rodeo held in Pocatello in March, the Riggins Rodeo in May, the Snake River Stampede and Nampa Good Old Dayz and Famous Preston Night Rodeo in July, the Shoshone-Bannock Indian Festival in August at Fort Hall, the Eastern Idaho State Fair in Blackfoot and the Lewiston Roundup in September.

Here's a cowboy gettin' ready to ride! Label the parts of his clothing, using the Word Bank below.

Word Bank

boots   chaps   gloves   hat   rope   saddle   stirrups   vest

Idaho Word Wheel

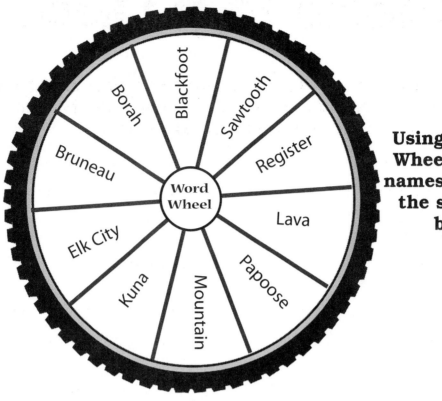

Word Wheel

Blackfoot · Sawtooth · Register · Lava · Borah · Bruneau · Elk City · Kuna · Mountain · Papoose

Using the Word Wheel of Idaho names, complete the sentences below.

1. The Idaho Champion Western Red Cedar Tree in __ __ __ __ __ __ __ is the largest tree in Idaho and is more than 3,000 years old.

2. __ __ __ __ __ __ __ Dunes State Park has North America's tallest single structured sand dune which is 470 feet (143 meters) tall.

3. __ __ __ __ is the gateway city to the Birds of Prey Natural Area.

4. The mineral pools that overlook the Portneuf River in __ __ __ __ Hot Springs are more than 50 million years old.

5. Pioneers used axle grease or knives to put their names on __ __ __ __ __ __ __ __ __ Rock in Massacre Rocks State Park.

6. __ __ __ __ __ __ __ Cave in the Seven Devils Mountains is one of the 10 deepest caverns in the United States.

7. __ __ __ __ __ __ __ __ Home Air Force Appreciation Day has the largest parade in Idaho every year.

8. Its jagged profile gave __ __ __ __ __ __ __ __ Mountain its name.

9. Mackay calls itself the "Top of Idaho" because it is the closest city to __ __ __ __ __ Peak.

10. __ __ __ __ __ __ __ __ __ is home to the Eastern Idaho State Fair.

Idaho Pop Quiz!

**Pop quiz! It's time to test your knowledge of Idaho!
Try to answer all of the questions before
you look at the answers.**

1. Idaho's nickname is the
   a) Evergreen State
   b) Sunshine State
   c) Gem State

2. Idaho became a territory in
   a) 1863
   b) 1889
   c) 1860

3. Idaho's state bird is the
   a) willow goldfinch
   b) mountain bluebird
   c) cardinal

4. Idaho's state insect is the
   a) monarch butterfly
   b) honeybee
   c) swallowtail butterfly

5. Idaho's capital city is
   a) Bismarck
   b) Olympia
   c) Boise

6. Idaho's state horse is the
   a) palomino
   b) appaloosa
   c) nokota

7. Idaho's state gem is the
   a) star sapphire
   b) star ruby
   c) star garnet

8. Idaho's state fish is the
   a) cutthroat trout
   b) sockeye salmon
   c) white sturgeon

9. Idaho's state flower is the
   a) white carnation
   b) white rose
   c) white syringa

10. Idaho's state folk dance is the
    a) swing
    b) waltz
    c) square dance

ANSWERS: 1-c; 2-a; 3-b; 4-a; 5-c; 6-b; 7-c; 8-a; 9-c; 10-c

Beautiful Bear Lake!

Soluable carbonates (minerals that can dissolve in water), especially limestone particles, give Bear Lake its beautiful turquoise water. The lake, which is 20 miles (32 kilometers) long and 7 miles (11 kilometers) wide, is shared by Idaho and Utah. Bear Lake is home to the Bear Lake monster, a creature with a serpent's body and horse's head! Native Americans told stories about the legendary creature to Idaho's settlers.

Bear Lake is also home to several species of fish that aren't found anywhere else! The best known of these species is the Bonneville cisco, a silvery whitefish which swims in schools beneath the ice. The lake's elevation is 5,923 feet (1,805 meters) so the water usually freezes. Fishermen cut holes in the ice and use buckets or nets to catch the sardine-like fish which is only about seven inches (17.8 centimeters) long.

In each pair of sentences below, one of the statements is false. Read them carefully and choose the sentence that is not true. Cross out the false sentence, and circle the true sentence.

1. The Bonneville cisco is a sardine-like fish that is found only in Bear Lake.

   The Bonneville cisco is a trout-like fish that is found only in Bear Lake.

2. Bear Lake's color is from silver deposits found beneath the water.

   Bear Lake's color is from soluble carbonates in the water.

3. Bear Lake is shared between Idaho and Wyoming.

   Idaho and Utah share Bear Lake.

4. Because of Bear Lake's elevation, the water usually freezes.

   Because of Bear Lake's elevation, the water is very hot.

5. Bear Lake is home to the legendary Bear Lake Monster.

   Bear Lake is home to the legendary Sasquatch.

ANSWERS: (Answers indicate false sentences) 1-second; 2-first; 3-first; 4-second; 5-second

An Abundance of Altitude!

With so many mountain ranges, Idaho has many peaks that offer great views. The highest point in the state is Borah Peak in the Lost River Range at 12,662 feet (3,859.4 meters). Hyndman Peak in the Sawtooth and Pioneer mountains reaches 12,078 feet (3,859 meters). Also located in the Sawtooth range is Bald Mountain in Sun Valley. When the first Sun Valley ski resort was built, "Baldy" was considered too big at 9,150 feet (2,789 meters) and too challenging in the 1930s.

The summit of Brundage Mountain in Seven Devils Mountains is 7,000 feet (2,134 meters). Mount Pulaski in the Bitterroot Range measures 5,480 feet (1,670 meters), and Kellogg Peak reaches 6,300 feet (1,920 meters).

Using the information in the paragraphs above, graph the heights of the different things listed. The first one has been done for you.

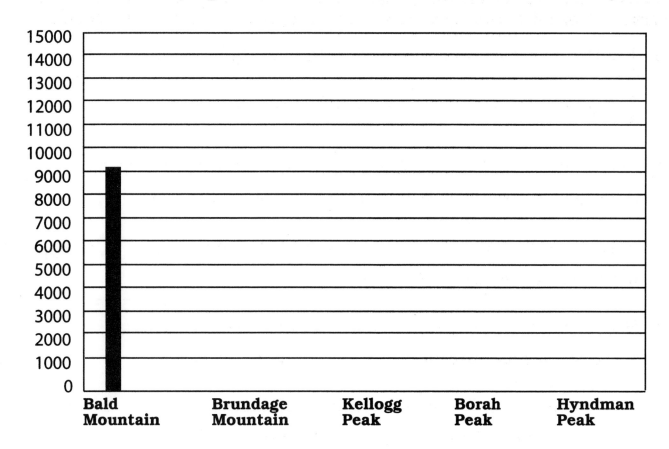

Stunning Shoshone Falls!

Shoshone Falls has been called one of the most stunning sights in Idaho! Located about 5 miles (8 kilometers) from Twin Falls, Shoshone Falls is also called the "Niagara of the West." The falls cascade 212 feet (65 meters)-45 feet (14 meters) higher than Niagara Falls. Shoshone Falls are shaped like a horseshoe and are 1,000 feet (305 meters) wide.

A haiku is a three-line poem with a certain number of syllables in each line. Look at the example below:

The first line has 5 syllables
Tall Sho/sho/ne Falls

The second line has 7 syllables
Ni/a/gar/a of the West

The third line has 5 syllables
Spec/tac/u/lar plunge!

Now, write your own haiku about the amazing Shoshone Falls!

_____

_____

_____

The Balancing Rock!

   The Salmon Falls Creek Canyon, south of Buhl, is home to the world-famous Balanced Rock. The rock is over 48 feet (14.6 meters) tall and balances on a pedestal that measures 3 feet (.9 meters) by 17 inches (43 centimeters). It weighs 40 tons (36 metric tons).
   According to geologists, the mushroom-shaped (or does it look more like a question mark?) boulder has been balancing on top of a larger rock for thousands of years. Its base is now reinforced with concrete!

Below is a picture of the Balanced Rock. Using the information above, label how tall it is, and how tall its pedestal is, in feet. Write how heavy the Balanced Rock is, in pounds.

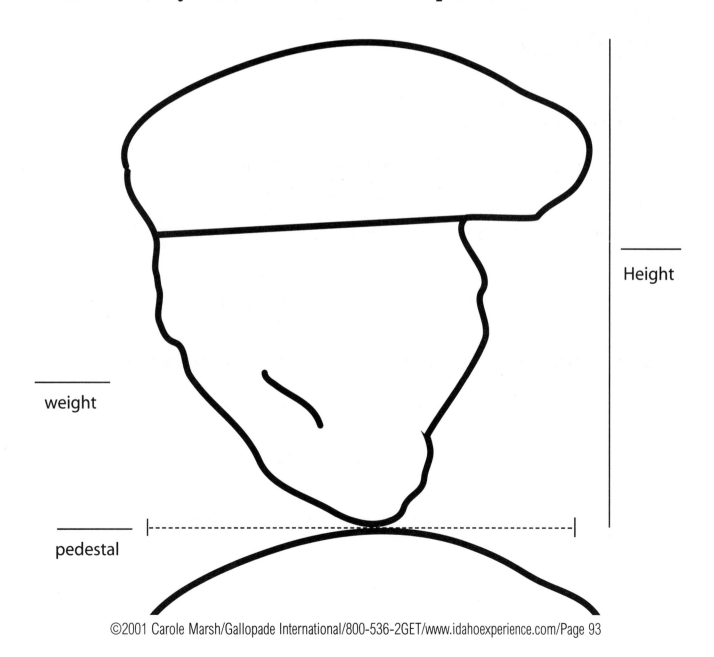

Height

weight

pedestal

How Big is Idaho?

Idaho is the 14th largest state in the United States. It has an area of approximately 83,574 square miles (216,440 square kilometers).

Can you answer the following questions?

1. How many states are there in the United States?

   _____

2. This many states are smaller than our state:

   _____

3. This many states are larger than our state:

   _____

4. One mile = 5,280 ____ ____ ____ ____

   HINT:

5. Draw a square foot.

6. Classroom Challenge: After you have drawn a square foot, measure the number of square feet in your classroom. Most floor tiles are square feet (12 inches by 12 inches). How many square feet are in your classroom? _____

   Bonus: Try to calculate how many classrooms would fit in the total area of your state. _____

   Hint: About 46,464 average classrooms would fit in just one square mile!

Celebrating the Capitol Building!

It took 15 years to construct Idaho's state capitol building in Boise! Construction started in 1905 and was completed in 1920 at a cost of $2.3 million. The capitol is modeled after the U.S. Capitol in Washington, D.C., and was designed by J.E. Tourtelloutte. Unlike the U.S. capitol, Idaho's capitol is heated by geothermal heat. Geothermal heat comes from the earth, and the capitol is heated by hot water from well located five blocks away.

A case in the capitol building displays the only remaining state seal of original design. Emma Edwards Green designed the seal in 1891. A statue of George Washington sitting on his horse is displayed in the same case. Charles Ostner created the statue. It took Ostner four years to carve the statue out of a single piece of yellow pine! Ostner bronzed the statue and gave it to the Idaho territorial government in 1869. The statue stood outside on the capitol grounds until 1934. The weather-damaged statue was covered in gold leaf and moved indoors!

1. Who designed the Idaho state capitol?

_____

2. How is the Idaho capitol building heated?

_____

3. When was construction of the capitol building completed?

_____

4. Who carved the statue of George Washington displayed in the capitol building?

_____

5. What kind of wood was used for the statue?

_____

ANSWERS: (Answers may vary.) 1- J.E. Tourtelloutte; 2-with geothermal heat; 3-1920; 4-Charles Ostner; 5-yellow pine

Idealic Idaho!

The words below are known as an acrostic. See if you can make up your own acrostic poem describing Idaho. **For each letter in Idaho's name, write down a word or phrase that describes Idaho. The first is done for you.**

I **is for Indian Valley!**

D is for _____

A is for _____

H is for _____

O is for _____

T is for _____

H is for _____

E is for _____

G is for _____

E is for _____

M is for _____

S is for _____

T is for _____

A is for _____

T is for _____

E is for _____